KNOW ABOUT
THE UNIVERSE

By

T. R. BHANOT

Illustrations

LAKSHYA ART STUDIO

DREAMLAND
PUBLICATIONS

First published in 1995 by
Dreamland Publications
J-128, Kirti Nagar, New Delhi- 110 015 (India)
Fax : 011-543 8283, Tel.: 011-543 5657

ISBN 81-7301-179-6
Processing :
Best Photo Lithographers

Printed at :
GRAPHO PRINT PROCESS

INTRODUCTION

The universe is limitless, edgeless and unending as well as ever-expanding. It has millions of star-systems including our star-system—*The Milky Way.* Our *solar-system* is only a very small part of our galaxy---the Milky Way---and our home-planet—*Earth*—in its turn is a very small part of the solar-system.

Evidently, our earth when compared to the universe at large is just as a *pebble* to a huge *mountain.*

Isn't it a matter to be utterly curious to know about the colossal universe— its *origin, shape, limit, contents, behaviour* etc. ? Certainly it is.

It is all these aspects of the universe that this book deals with ; but in detail just sufficient for upcoming children and for the common man. Attractive illustrations are there to help grasping of the facts so that they may go quite home.

After knowing all about the universe, one is sure to feel fuller and better-informed about something that is really fantastic. Won't it be a matter to feel proud of being a part of such an immense entity ?

—AUTHOR

CONTENTS

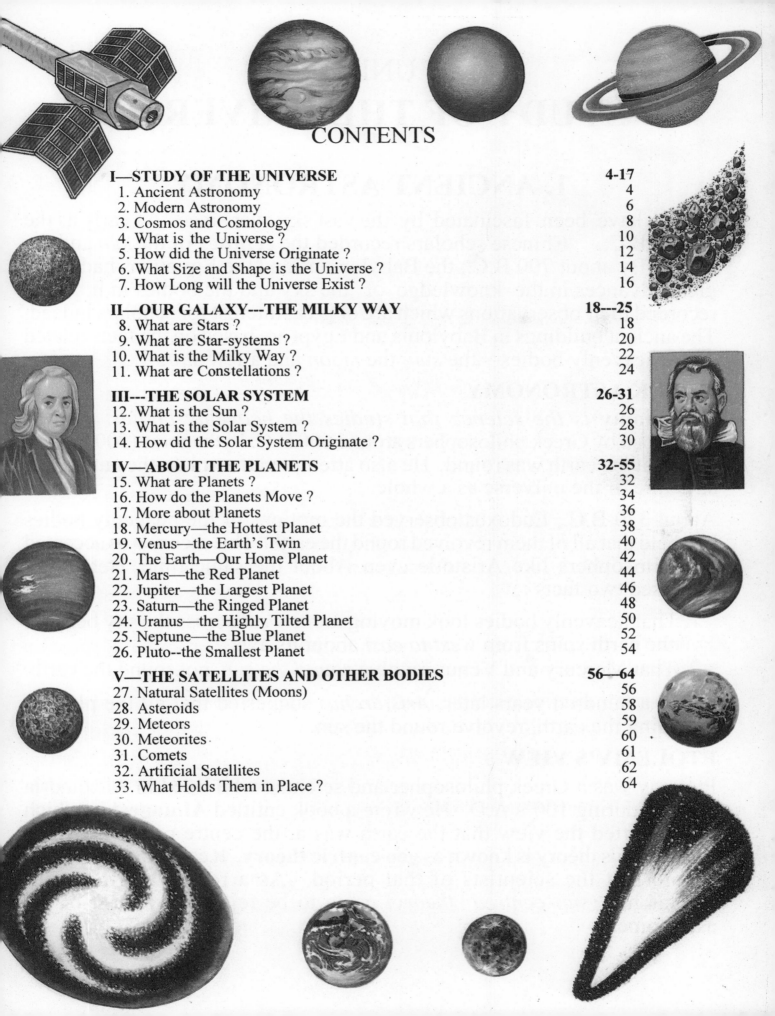

UNIT I
STUDY OF THE UNIVERSE

1. ANCIENT ASTRONOMY

People have been fascinated by the vast sky ever since. As early as the 1300's B.C., Chinese scholars recorded the *eclipses* of the *sun* and the *moon*. By about 700 B.C., the Babylonians and the Egyptians had made great advances in the knowledge of the sky and the bodies in it. They recorded their observations which are of great interest for scholars indeed. The ancient buildings in Babylonia and Egypt are based on the facts related to the heavenly bodies—the *sun,* the *moon* and a few *stars.*

GREEK ASTRONOMY

Astronomy *is the science that studies the heavenly bodies.* It was developed by Greek philosophers around 600 B.C. Pythagoras (500 B.C.'s) held that the earth was round. He also attempted to explain the nature and structure of the universe as a whole.

About 370 B.C., Eudoxus observed the motions of the heavenly bodies and held that all of them revolved round the earth. This theory was accepted by philosophers like Aristotle even. About the same time, Heraclides proposed two facts :

1. That heavenly bodies look moving *to the west* across the sky because the earth spins from *west to east* about its axis.
2. That Mercury and Venus revolve *round the sun*, not round the earth.

About a hundred years later, *Aristarchus* suggested that all the planets, including the earth, revolve round the sun.

PTOLEMY'S VIEW

Ptolemy was a Greek philosopher and scientist who lived in Alexandria (Egypt) during 100's A.D. He wrote a book entitled **Almagest** in which he supported the view that the earth was at the centre of the heavenly system. This theory is known as **geo-centric theory.** It came to be accepted by most of the scientists of that period. As a result, the theory of Aristarchus (*sun-centred theory*) came to be rejected by most of the astronomers.

PYTHAGORAS

ARISTARCHUS

ARISTOTLE

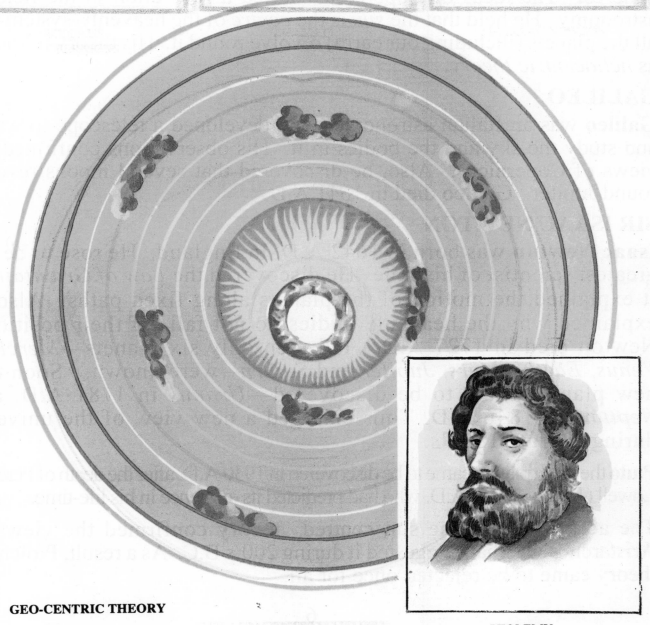

GEO-CENTRIC THEORY

PTOLEMY

2. MODERN ASTRONOMY

Ptolemy's theory continued to be accepted for about 1500 years. Throughout this period, Europeans paid little attention to astronomy, though most of the scholars questioned the views of Ptolemy when the Latin translation of his book—*Almagest*—reached Europe. But no one could muster up courage to challenge it openly.

NICOLAUS COPERNICUS

Finally **Nicolaus Copernicus**, a Polish scientist, made a breakthrough in 1543 A.D. through his book–*Concerning the Revolutions of the Celestial Spheres*. The ideas of Copernicus caused a revolution in the field of astronomy. He held that the *sun* is the *centre* of the heavenly-system and all the planets (including our earth) revolve round it. His theory is known as *heliocentric theory*.

GALILEO

Galileo was an Italian astronomer who developed a telescope to watch and study the sky and the bodies in it. His observations confirmed the views of Copernicus. Also, he discovered that several moons revolve round Jupiter. Galileo died in 1641 A.D.

SIR ISAAC NEWTON

Isaac Newton was born in 1642 A.D. in England. He rose to be the greatest scientist of his time. He discovered the *Law of Gravitation*. It explained the motion of the planets along fixed paths. Also, it explained why the heavenly bodies do not fall off their positions. Newton died in 1727 A.D. Till then only six planets—*Mercury, Venus, Earth, Mars, Jupiter* and *Saturn*—were known. Soon two new planets came to be discovered—*Uranus* in 1781 A.D. and *Neptune* in 1846 A.D. Thus emerged a new view of the universe during the late 1800's.

Pluto the ninth planet, came to be discovered in 1930 A.D. after the death of Percival Lowell (1855—1916) A.D. who had predicted its existence in his life-time.

The acceptance of the sun-centred theory confirmed the views of Aristarchus who had suggested it during 200's B.C. As a result, Ptolemy's theory came to be rejected once for all.

NICOLAUS COPERNICUS

GALILEO

SIR ISAAC NEWTON

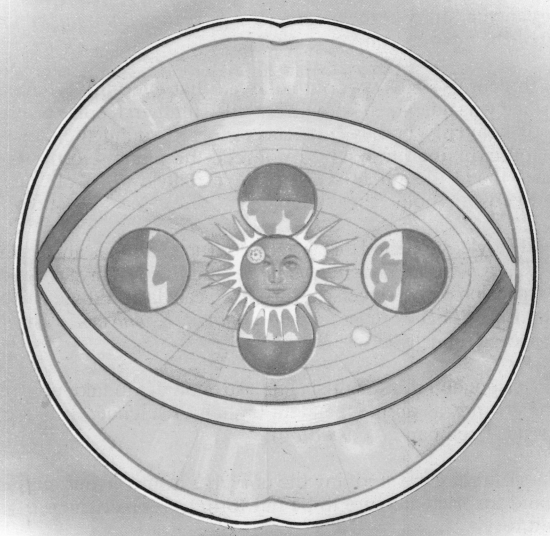

THE SUN-CENTRED THEORY

3. COSMOS AND COSMOLOGY

THE COSMOS

Cosmos is a term used in astronomy as well as physics. It refers to everything that exists—from the smallest atoms to the huge heavenly bodies that are far away from us. This word has come down from the ancient Greek word—*kosmos*—which means *well-ordered universe* or *world*. The Greeks believed that cosmos was a homogeneous (uniform) system consisting of the earth, the sun, the moon, stars, and other visible planets. But today we know that the cosmos is far more larger than the one that the ancient people thought it to be. The term *cosmos* is another word for **universe** indeed.

COSMOLOGY

Cosmology means study of the *origin, structure, development, behaviour* and *future* of the cosmos (universe).

Till the 17th century A.D., people believed that everything beyond the earth's surface was not worth knowing at all. But then Kepler proved that a number of heavenly bodies (planets) revolved round the sun. Also, Isaac Newton explained how gravity forced the planets to move along fixed paths. It led the scientists to believe that laws of physics were applicable to cosmic bodies as well.

In 1915, Fred Hoyle, suggested that the cosmos (universe) has always existed. *New matter keeps being created out of nothing* to fill the empty spaces caused due to the expansion of the universe. But a few years later, Edwin Hubble put forth the **Big Bang Theory** regarding the *origin of the universe*. This theory came to be accepted finally before long.

These theories goaded the scientists and astronomers to take up a regular study of the cosmos as an independent branch of science. It is this very branch that has been named *cosmology.*

Astronomers of today are studying the universe from various angles. So, new facts and theories are sure to be put forth to replace the old ones in the near future.

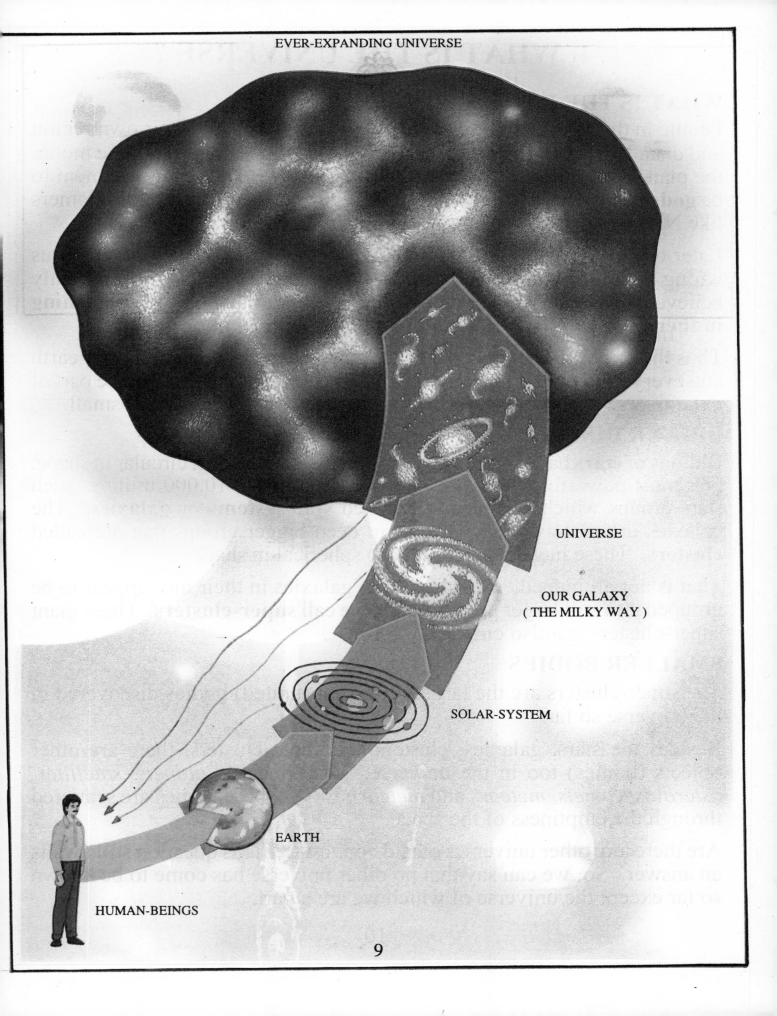

UNIVERSE

OUR GALAXY
(THE MILKY WAY)

SOLAR-SYSTEM

EARTH

HUMAN-BEINGS

4. WHAT IS THE UNIVERSE ?

WHAT IS THE UNIVERSE ?

People in the past thought that the *universe* consisted of their own region and distant places which they had heard of along with the sun, the moon, the planets and stars. As for the heavenly bodies, they believed them to be **gods** and **spirits.** It was during the 1400's and 1500's that astronomers like Nicolaus Copernicus made new discoveries.

Later on, the invention of Galileo's telescope shattered all the previous wrong beliefs about the universe and its behaviour. Today, it is rightly believed that the **universe is the whole of space and time and everything in them**—*matter, light* and *all other forms of radiation* and *energy.*

Thus the universe includes the entire solar system—along with our earth and everything on it. All the stars (our sun is one of these stars) are part of the universe too. The bodies in the universe are big as well as small.

BIGGER BODIES

Billions of **stars** have formed large groups that are almost circular in shape. Our most powerful telescopes have located at least 10,000 million such stars-groups which are generally called **star-systems** or **galaxies.** The galaxies in the universe tend to form even bigger groups that are called **clusters.** These huge clusters are also spherical in shape.

That is not all indeed. The clusters of galaxies in their turn appear to be grouped into still larger groups which we call **super-clusters.** These giant super-clusters are also circular in form.

SMALLER BODIES

The super-clusters are the largest coherent (united) bodies discovered in the universe so far.

Besides the stars, galaxies, clusters and super-clusters, there are other objects (bodies) too in the universe. They include *planets, satellites, asteroids, comets, meteors* and *meteorites.* All these bodies are scattered through the emptiness of the space.

Are there any other universes outside our own ? This question still awaits an answer. So, we can say that no other universe has come to be known so far except the universe of which we are a part.

FRED HOYLE

GALILEO'S TELESCOPE

EDWIN HUBBLE

COSMOS

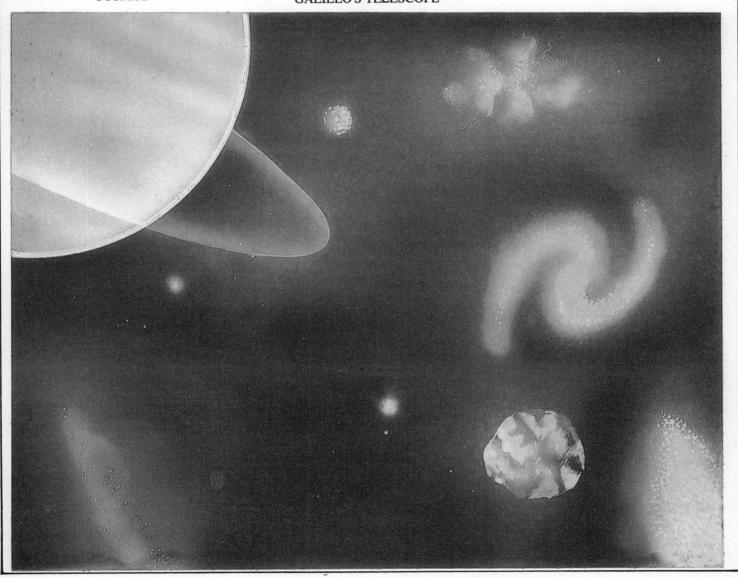

5. HOW DID THE UNIVERSE ORIGINATE ?

Scientists differ on how the universe had its origin. Some of them believe that matter has always kept being created in a regular way. So, we can say that the universe must have had its origin a long, long time—billions of years—ago. This theory does not explain what the source of all the matter of the universe was. As this theory holds that the universe is steady (not moving), it has been given the name---*Steady State Theory*.

But most scientists support the view that the universe had its origin as a result of a gigantic explosion. This view has been given the name—*Big-Bang Theory*.

THE BIG BANG

Out of the two theories regarding the origin of the universe, the *Big Bang Theory* has been accepted all over. But no one knows why the Big Bang took place. As for the other theory, it has not been accepted because it fails to explain the source of all the matter that is there in the universe.

This *Big Bang* is believed to have occurred 10 to 20 billion years ago and resulted in the beginning of the universe. The *then universe* consisted of strong radiation which soon took the shape of a **fire-ball.**

The fire-ball began to expand at a quick rate and within a few hundred years, a major part of the expanding ball took the form of matter. The matter consisted mainly of **hydrogen gas** with a small amount of **helium** and some other light elements. As a result, the radiation went on becoming thinner and thinner. And today, *only faint radio-waves* are all that exists out of the original radiation.

In due course, the matter broke apart into big lumps which formed **galaxies.** In their turn, the galaxies broke apart to form **stars.**

As for the galaxy that we live in, at least one lump broke apart to form *the sun, all the planets, satellites, asteroids* etc. that constitute our **solar-system.**

Evidently, our solar-system is a very small part of the universe. As for our earth, it forms a still smaller part of it.

THE
BIG BANG

6. WHAT SIZE AND SHAPE IS THE UNIVERSE ?

SIZE OF THE UNIVERSE

No one knows about the limits of the universe. But all the scientists agree on the point that the universe has been expanding ever since its origin. Also, it still does continue to do so. The galaxy-clusters are flying further apart. As a result, the universe is getting larger and larger day after day.

The fact that the universe is constantly expanding was established by an American astronomer named *Edwin Hubble* (1889-1953) A.D. In 1920's he studied hundreds of distant galaxies and classified them into various types. Also, he measured the shift in their brightness and proved that they are moving away from one another very rapidly.

Apart from the galaxies, a new type of objects has come to be discovered in the universe. These objects look like stars which they are actually not. So, these objects have been named **quasars.** The first quasar was discovered in the year 1960 A.D. Hundreds of them have been located through optical and radio telescopes by now. These quasars are believed to be the most distant objects in the universe. So, the universe is limitless and endless. Its size cannot be described in any measurements — *length,width* or *area* etc.

SHAPE OF THE UNIVERSE

To say that *the universe is getting larger and larger*, does not mean that it has an *edge*. The universe has no edge at all. Trying to find the edge of the universe is just like trying to find the *end* of a circle. Evidently, the universe is *spherical in shape*.

The word---*spherical*---does not mean *an exact circle* here. It simply points to the fact that the universe has no end or edge just as a circle doesn't have. We often say that *the earth is round* in shape. But actually it is bulged out at the equator and a bit flattened at either pole. So, it is more like a pear or an orange. Somewhat similar seems to be the case with the universe. As the universe is endless, its photographs cannot be taken unless one (the photographer with his device) gets out of it. But it is altogether impossible ; isn't it ?

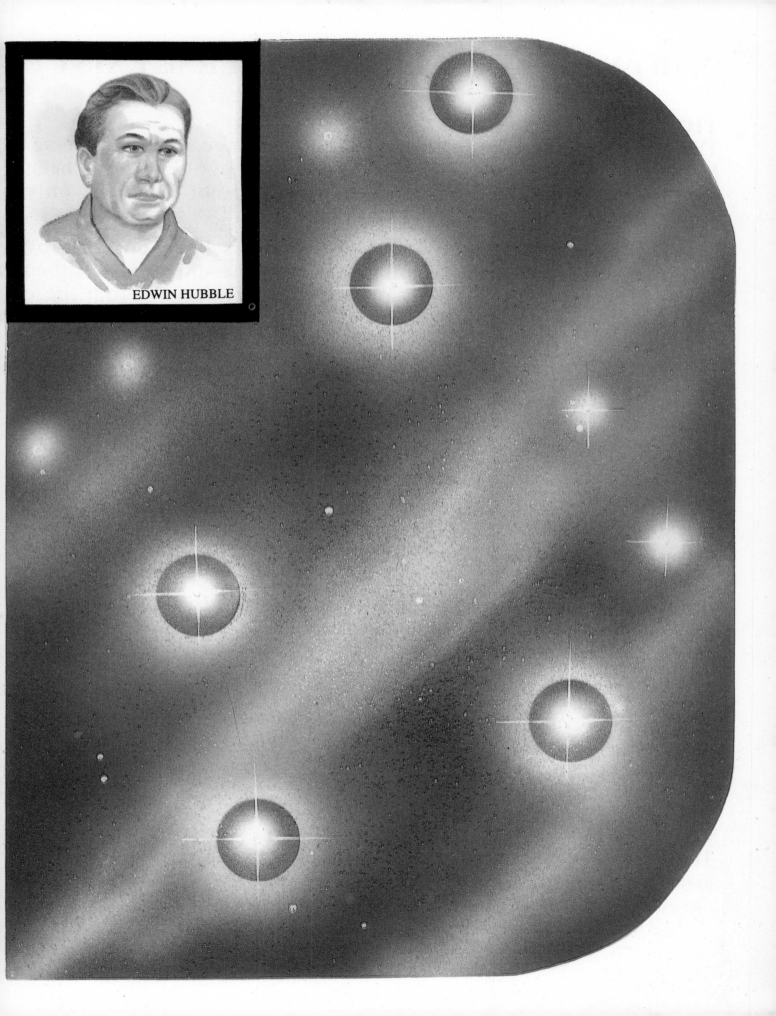

EDWIN HUBBLE

7. HOW LONG WILL THE UNIVERSE EXIST ?

THE BYGONE AGE

There is no method to determine the bygone age of the universe. Still the scientists have cleverly figured out how long it has been there. This age of the universe is, however, not exact but only approximate.

The estimate of the age of the universe has been possible by measuring speed of the stars in one part of the universe and then measuring speeds of the stars in other distant parts. From these speeds, the scientists could calculate the speed of the stars billions of years ago.

By comparing the present and old speeds of the stars, the scientists calculated when the stars had begun to move in space. In this way, they estimated that the universe is at least ten billion years old. It may be older/far older even. That is why its age is mentioned to be 10 to 20 billion years old.

FUTURE OF THE UNIVERSE

Scientists differ on how long the universe will exist. Some of them believe that it will go on for ever — even after all the stars have ceased to shine. They hold that the universe will be quite dark and cold then.

But other scientists believe that the universe will go on expanding, no doubt. But ultimately it will reach a stage where *further expansion* will not be possible. This stage will be followed by a period of *contraction* and the universe will reach its original state to repeat the process of expansion again. This theory has been named the **Oscillation Theory** because this behaviour of *expansion-contraction-expansion* (again) will resemble the oscillation of a clock-pendulum.

According to the *oscillation theory*, the universe will never cease to exist. It will keep expanding and contracting in turn again and again. Thus it will go on for all time to come.

The laws of physics are believed to be applicable to the universe. So, according to the law—*matter can never be destroyed* — the universe has to go on. The *theory of contraction* has been named--**Big Crunch Theory**.

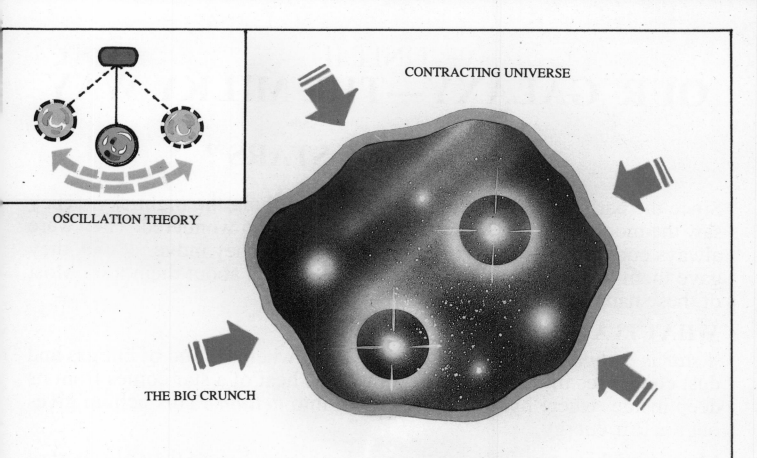

OSCILLATION THEORY

CONTRACTING UNIVERSE

THE BIG CRUNCH

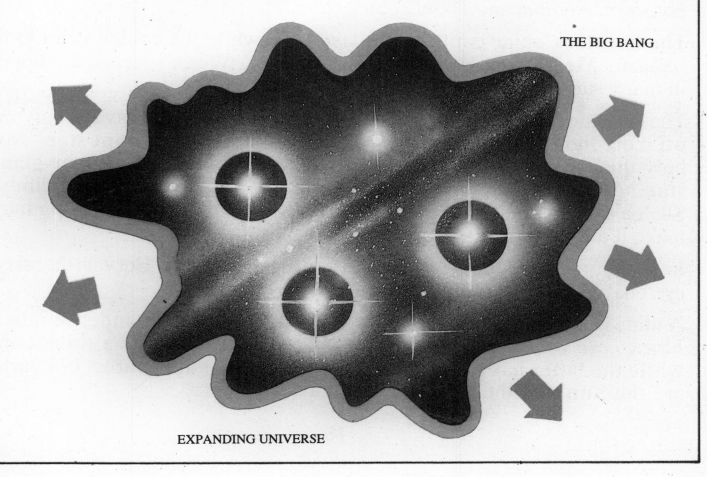

THE BIG BANG

EXPANDING UNIVERSE

UNIT II
OUR GALAXY—THE MILKY WAY

8. WHAT ARE STARS ?

Since the earliest time, people have been watching the night-sky. They saw the moon and stars moving across the sky and wondered. They were always curious to know what they are and why they move.   So, they gave them names and made up interesting stories about them too. Most of these names are *Greek, Indian* and *Arabic.*

WHAT IS A STAR ?

A star is a shining ball of gas. It is formed when a cloud of hot gas and dust condenses into a globe-like form. The heat of a star comes from its deep inside where hydrogen has turned into *helium.* This helium gives out nuclear energy.

Most stars shine regularly for thousands of years before they run short of fuel and extinguish. Stars can be classified into three chief groups—*very hot stars, medium stars* and *cooler stars.*

The **hot stars** shine emitting a *bluish light* while the **cooler stars** look *reddish.* **Medium stars** look *yellow* in colour. We can see these colours in many stars that can be seen with the naked eye.

The colour of a star tells a lot about it. Sometimes a star may start giving off more light and grow into a red, yellow or even blue **giant star**. Not only this, it may grow even larger and hotter to become a **super-giant star**. A star that loses its energy and shrinks in size, shines only dimly. Such a star is called a **white-dwarf.** Further shrinking and cooling may make it a **black dwarf.**

In all, there are at least 100,000 million stars in our star-system. But with the naked eye, one can see about 3000 stars at one time.

A star, if it explodes, is called a **supernova.** It may condense into a *black hole* or a *neutron star* (pulsar). The former has a thick core while the latter has a thinner one. Two stars that are nearest our earth are the **Sun** and the **Proxima Centauri.**

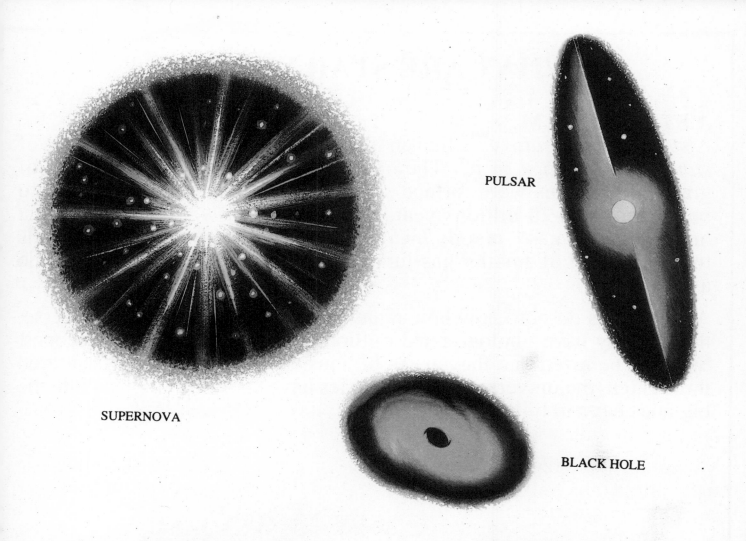

SUPERNOVA

PULSAR

BLACK HOLE

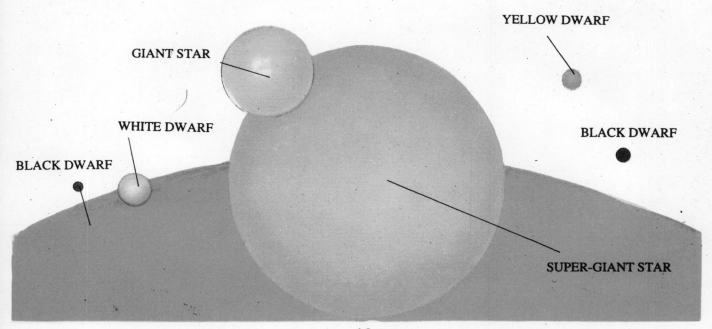

GIANT STAR

YELLOW DWARF

WHITE DWARF

BLACK DWARF

BLACK DWARF

SUPER-GIANT STAR

9. WHAT ARE STAR-SYSTEMS ?

A STAR SYSTEM

A **star-system** *(galaxy)* is like an independent star-city with millions of *stars, gas* and *dust* in it. They are all held together by the force of gravity. Galaxies were formed soon after the universe had come into being about 10-20 billions years ago. To begin with, they were just huge clouds of gas—mainly *hydrogen*. By and by the huge gas-clouds took the shape of smaller gas-lumps due to gravity and began to shine as stars.

Astronomers do not know how many galaxies there are in the universe, though they have photographed millions of them with their telescopes. Still it is believed that they are in billions. They are unevenly scattered throughout the universe. Small galaxies have stars in millions while the big ones have in billions and trillions.

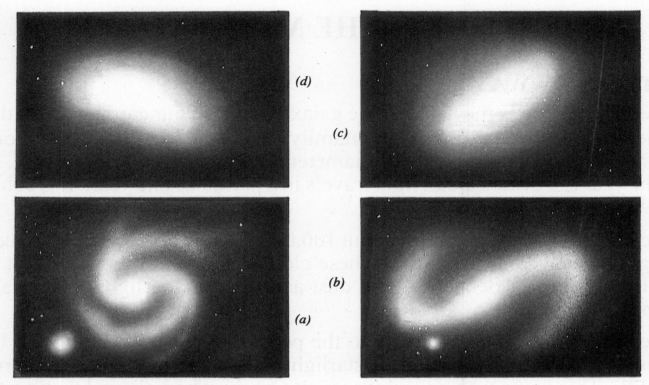

(d)

(c)

(b)

(a)

TYPES OF GALAXIES

The galaxy, whereof our solar system is a part, is called the **Milky Way.** Besides it, three other galaxies can be seen from the earth with the naked eye on dark clear nights. They are :

1. **Andromeda** which can be seen in the northern hemisphere,
2. **Large Magellanic Cloud,**   They can be seen in the southern
3. **Small Magellanic Cloud**   hemisphere

Galaxies fall into four types in respect of their shapes :

(a) Spiral (Disc) Galaxies   (b) Barred Spiral (Disc) Galaxies

(c) Elliptical Galaxies   (d) Irregular Galaxies

The pictures given above show all these shapes clearly.

Galaxies occur in small and big clusters that may number in two or three digits. These clusters may belong to super-clusters. These clusters and super-clusters are speedily flying away from one another because the universe is ever-expanding.

Galaxies give off several kinds of radiation (light rays etc.) in space. Some scientists believe that all galaxies are about the same age as they were formed soon after the *Big Bang.* But others believe that new galaxies keep forming constantly as the old ones move apart.

10. WHAT IS THE MILKY WAY ?

THE MILKY WAY

The **Milky Way** is the name of the galaxy in which our earth, with all the other members of the solar(sun's)family, is located. In other words, our galaxy is enormous in size. Its diameter is about 100,000 *light-years*. A light-year is a distance that light travels in a period of one year. It is equal to 946 trillion kilometers.

The Milky Way is made up of about 100,000 million stars and huge clouds of gas as well as dust. Each of these clouds along with the stars in it is called a **nebula**. Because of the dust and the gas, the light of the stars appears to be faint.

The name—*Milky Way*—refers to the portion of the galaxy that can be seen as a broad milky band of starlight across the sky on clear starry nights. This name was given by ancient Greeks who believed that it was formed by the drops of milk that dripped from the breasts of goddess Hera--wife of Zeus, chief of the gods. We, in India, call it *Aakash Ganga* while the Arabians call it *Kahkashaan*.

The Milky Way is a spiral galaxy shaped like a disc. It has a bulge in the centre from which fan out long curved arms to form its spiral. The inner bulge contains

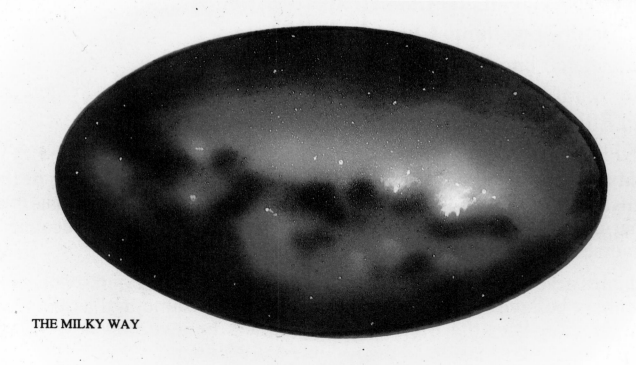

THE MILKY WAY

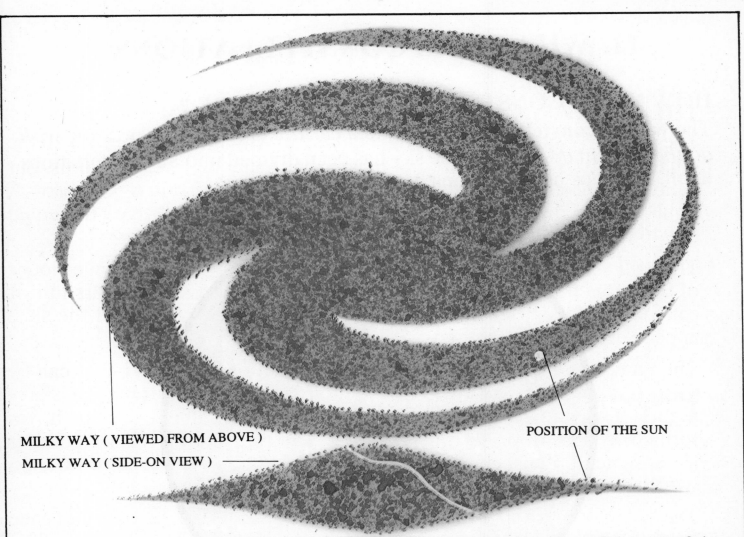

MILKY WAY (VIEWED FROM ABOVE)

MILKY WAY (SIDE-ON VIEW) ─────────

POSITION OF THE SUN

most of the older stars while the younger ones lie in the outer flat part of the galaxy. These young stars, along with the gas and the dust present there, form the **halo** around the central bulge.

SHAPE OF THE MILKY WAY

The Milky Way is shaped liked a flat spiral of stars. Some parts of this galaxy are so thick with stars that they have taken a cloudy appearance. Note that the bright streak shown in the picture given above) is the track of an artificial satellite launched into the sky.

The Milky Way consists of several spiral arms that contain millions of *nebulae*.

All the stars and the star-clusters in the Milky Way revolve round its centre just as our earth and other planets revolve about the sun. Our sun is about 30,000 light-years away from the centre of the Milky Way and thus lies in its outer part.

11. WHAT ARE CONSTELLATIONS ?

HOW MANY CONSTELLATIONS ARE THERE ?

The word—**constellation**—refers to a *certain area of the sky along with all the stars in it.* Till now the sky has been divided into 88 constellations in all. Various constellations have different shapes.

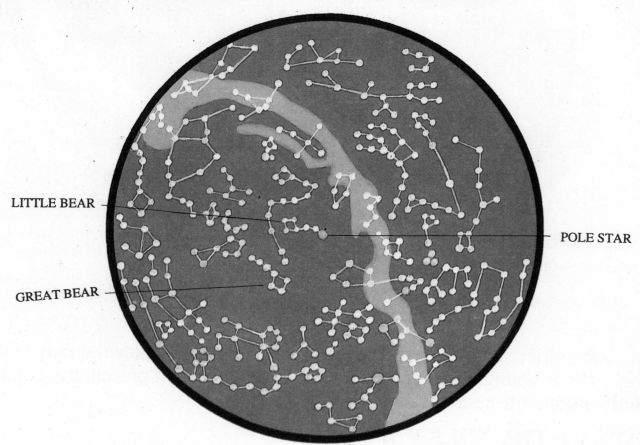

LITTLE BEAR

GREAT BEAR

POLE STAR

To begin with, ancient Babylonians discovered 12 constellations that are the basis of astrology. These twelve constellations were named during 2500-2000 B.C.

Later on, the Greek and the Roman astronomers observed a number of more constellations in the two-thirds of the northern sky and named them after *animals* and *mythological characters.* By the time of Ptolemy (100's A.D.), the number of known constellations had reached 48.

Between 1400's and 1700's European sailors explored the southern seas and observed more constellations in the one-third of the remaining (southern) sky. These constellations were named after scientific instruments, and animals. Thus the number of constellations came to be 88 in all.

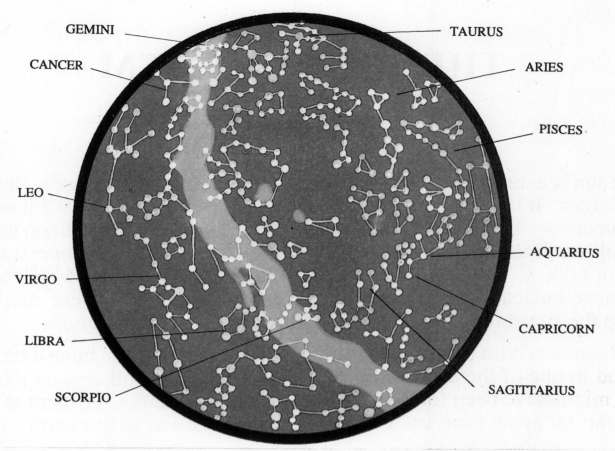

In some constellations, there are well- known groups of stars. These groups are called **asterisms**. The *big dipper* is an asterism in the constellation Ursa Major (Great Bear). *Little Dipper* is another asterism located in the Ursa Minor (Little Bear).

Remember that some of the 88 constellations can be seen only during certain periods of the year because of the revolution of the earth around the sun.

CONSTELLATIONS USED IN ASTROLOGY

The 12 constellations used in astrology are :

1. Aries (*Ram*) 2. Taurus(*Bull*) 3.Gemini (*Twins*)
4. Cancer(*Crab*) 5. Leo (*Lion*) 6.Virgo (*Virgin*)
7. Libra (*Scales*) 8. Scorpio (*Scorpion*) 9.Sagittarius (*Archer*)
10. Capricorn (*Goat*)11. Aquarius(*Water-carrier*)12.Pisces (*Fishes*)

THEIR SIGNS

The signs of the above-named twelve astrological constellations are as under :

1. ♈ 2. ♉ 3. ♊ 4. ♋ 5. ♌ 6. ♍
7. ♎ 8. ♏ 9. ♐ 10. ♑ 11. ♒ 12. ♓

UNIT III
THE SOLAR SYSTEM

12. WHAT IS THE SUN ?

The sun is a medium-sized star. It is a ball made up of hot gases—mostly *hydrogen*. It is very, very big in size having a diameter of 1392 thousand kilometres—1100 times the diameter of the Earth. So, its volume is over a million times the volume of the earth. It has a surface temperature of about 6000°C. But at its centre, the temperature is about 15 million °C because nuclear reactions are always going on there. These reactions keep the sun shining and it emits light and heat in all directions.

The sun was born about 4500 million years ago out of the huge dark gas-cloud in one of the arms of the Milky Way. Several other stars like the sun might have been formed at that time. But we cannot see them as they are far, far away from us. Our sun is the nearest star to our earth.

The sun has been losing its energy in the forms of **heat** and **light.** It has been through nearly half its life and the energy left with it is enough to keep it shining steadily for another 5000 million years.

Compared to other stars, the sun is smaller and dimmer. But as it is only 150 million kilometres away from us, it looks large and bright. Only a small part of the sun's energy reaches our earth. It is due to this energy that the earth is a liveable planet, with various living things on it.

The sun is roughly round in shape and has spots on it. These areas are comparatively cooler than other areas. So, they look as spots on the face of the sun. They are called **sun-spots.**

Huge streamers of glowing gas leap up from the sun's surface. They are like flames and are called **prominences.** Some of them curve to make *arcs of fire*. Moreover, atomic particles shoot in all directions from the sun at the speed of a bullet. They spread out very thinly. They are called **solar wind** which blows beyond Neptune even. The sun has three layers :

1. **Photosphere** : The shining surface that we see from the earth
2. **Chromosphere** : A layer some thousand km. below the photosphere
3. **Corona** : The atmosphere that stretches millions of km. around it

26

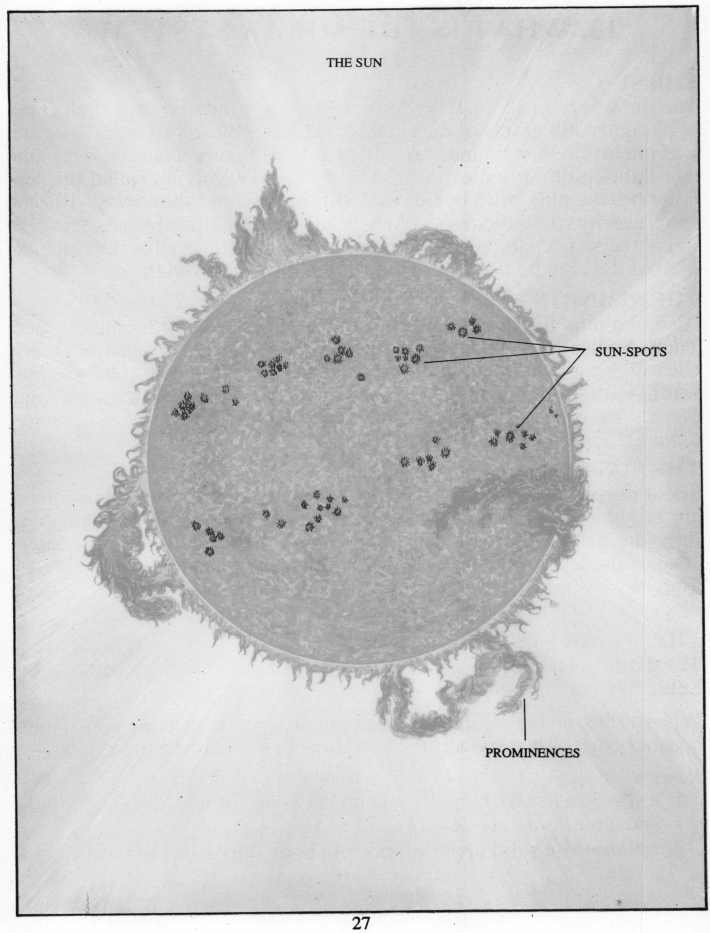

SUN-SPOTS

PROMINENCES

13. WHAT IS THE SOLAR SYSTEM ?

THE SUN

The sun was born about 4500 millions years ago out of a large dark cloud of gas and solid grains of dust condensed into a cluster of stars. The sun was one of these stars indeed. It had a disc of some material with nine non-light-emitting bodies in it. The disc was revolving round the sun. Later on, the nine solid bodies took off the disc and shot away. But the sun's gravity (pull) did not let them be all-free. So, they began to revolve round the sun separately along fixed paths (orbits). As for the distance, each of the nine bodies was at a different distance from the sun.

THE PLANETS

Also, the nine lightless bodies began to spin round and round in space. These bodies have been named **planets** (*wanderers*) by astronomers. Clearly, each planet had half of its surface facing the sun. So, this half was lit with sunlight while the other half was in starlit darkness. The nine planets have been named as—*Mercury, Venus, Earth, Mars, Jupiter, Saturn, Uranus, Neptune* and *Pluto*.

THE SUN'S FAMILY

Six of the planets—Mercury, Venus, Mars, Jupiter, Saturn and Uranus—are bright enough to be seen with the naked eye while the remaining three are visible through a telescope only. Also, there are millions of smaller bodies in the space through which the planets revolve (move). They are *moons, asteroids, comets, meteors* and *meteorites*. All these bigger and smaller bodies make the **sun's family** (*solar family*).

THE SOLAR SYSTEM

The entire solar family and the sun itself are together known as the **Solar System**.

Whereas the sun is a medium-sized shining star, the planets are non-shining opaque bodies. Their surfaces are lit with sunlight—half at a time.

Remember that—
1. a **star** is a heavenly body hot enough at its surface to shine brightly and emit *light-rays in space*.
2. a **planet** is a solid opaque heavenly body only half-lit by sunlight at a time.

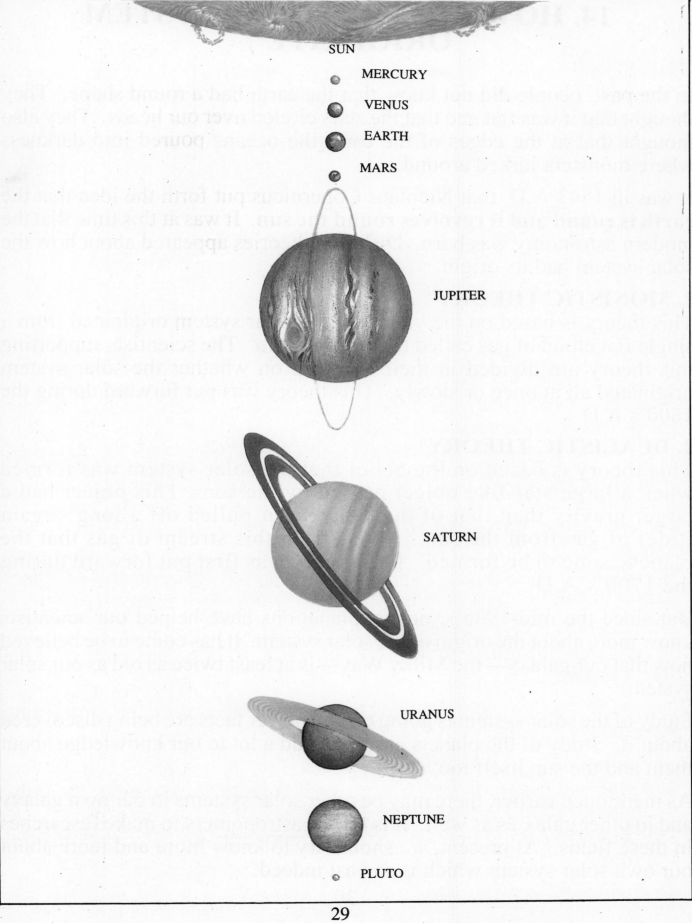

SUN

MERCURY

VENUS

EARTH

MARS

JUPITER

SATURN

URANUS

NEPTUNE

PLUTO

14. HOW DID THE SOLAR SYSTEM ORIGINATE ?

In the past, people did not know that the earth had a round shape. They thought that it was flat and that the stars circled over our heads. They also thought that at the edges of the earth the oceans poured into darkness where monsters lurked around.

It was in 1543 A.D. that Nicolaus Copernicus put forth the idea that the **earth is round and it revolves round the sun**. It was at this time that the modern astronomy was born. Different theories appeared about how the solar system had its origin.

1. MONISTIC THEORY

This theory is based on the view that the solar system originated from a single flat cloud of gas called the *solar nebula*. The scientists supporting this theory are divided in their opinions on whether the solar system originated all at once or slowly. This theory was put forward during the 1600's A.D.

2. DUALISTIC THEORY

This theory is based on the belief that the solar system was formed when a large star-like object passed by the sun. This object had a larger gravity than that of the sun. So, it pulled off a long stream (tide) of gas from the sun. It was from this stream of gas that the planets came to be formed. This theory was first put forward during the 1700's A.D.

But since the mid-1900's, new explanations have helped our scientists know more about the origin of the solar system. It has come to be believed now that our galaxy—the Milky Way—is at least twice as old as our solar system.

Study of the solar system is going on and newer facts are being discovered about it. Study of the planets is sure to add a lot to our knowledge about them and the sun itself too.

As mentioned earlier, there may be other solar systems in our own galaxy and in other galaxies as well. It is for the astronomers to make researches in these fields. At present, we should try to know more and more about our own solar system which is so vast indeed.

HOW THE SOLAR SYSTEM BEGAN

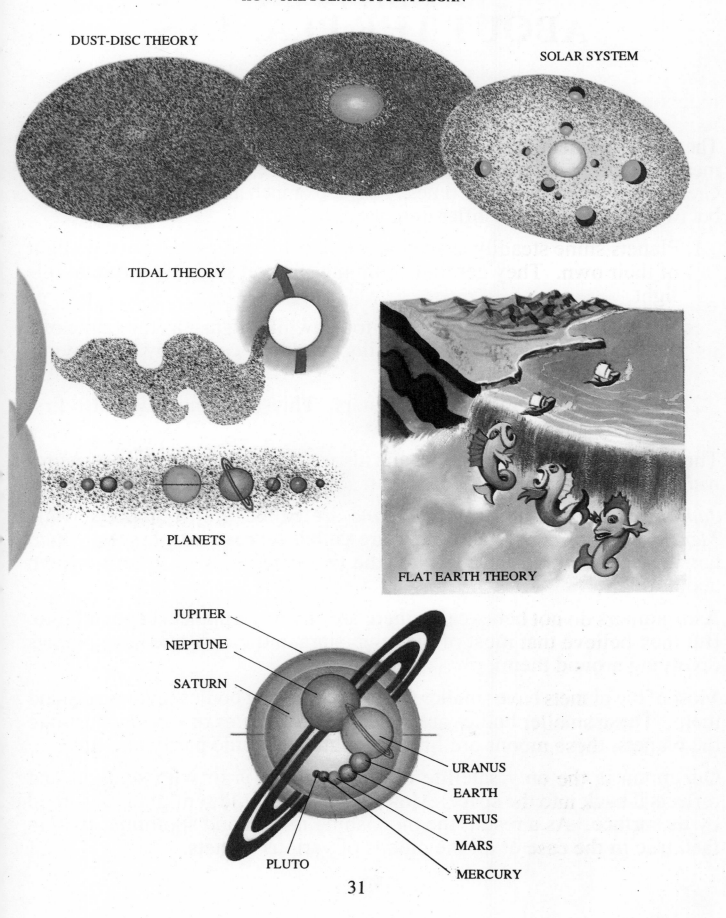

DUST-DISC THEORY

SOLAR SYSTEM

TIDAL THEORY

PLANETS

FLAT EARTH THEORY

JUPITER

NEPTUNE

SATURN

URANUS

EARTH

VENUS

MARS

MERCURY

PLUTO

UNIT IV
ABOUT THE PLANETS

15. WHAT ARE PLANETS ?

The word—**planet**—has come down from the Greek word—*planetes*—which means *wanderer*. Planets were first discovered to be different from the stars by Greek astronomers in ancient times. They look much like stars in the night-sky but two facts make them differ from the stars :

1. Planets shine steadily as they are dark solid bodies and have no light of their own. They get light from the sun and shine by virtue of this light.

   Stars, on the other hand, appear to be twinkling just as the flame of a candle flickers in light wind. This twinkle is caused by the moving air of the atmosphere.

2. Planets move in relation to the stars. This movement was also first noted by ancient Greek scholars.

The planets differ greatly in size and also in distance from the sun. As for *weight,* they together weigh less than a hundredth of the sun's weight.

Jupiter, Saturn, Uranus and *Neptune* are called **major planets** while *Mercury, Venus, Earth* and *Mars* are called **terrestrial planets.** *Pluto* has not yet been placed in any of the two categories as little is known about it.

Astronomers do not believe that there are any more planets beyond Pluto. But they believe that most of the other stars in the universe have planets revolving around them.

Most of the planets have smaller non-light-emitting bodies revolving round them. These smaller bodies are called their *satellites* or *moons*. Just like the planets, these moons are lit by sunlight and shine partly at a time.

Our moon is the only satellite of our earth. It is lit with sunlight and reflects it back into the space. Most of the heat of the sunlight is absorbed by its surface. As a result, the moonshine is cool and soothing. It is, in fact, true in the case of all the moons of various planets.

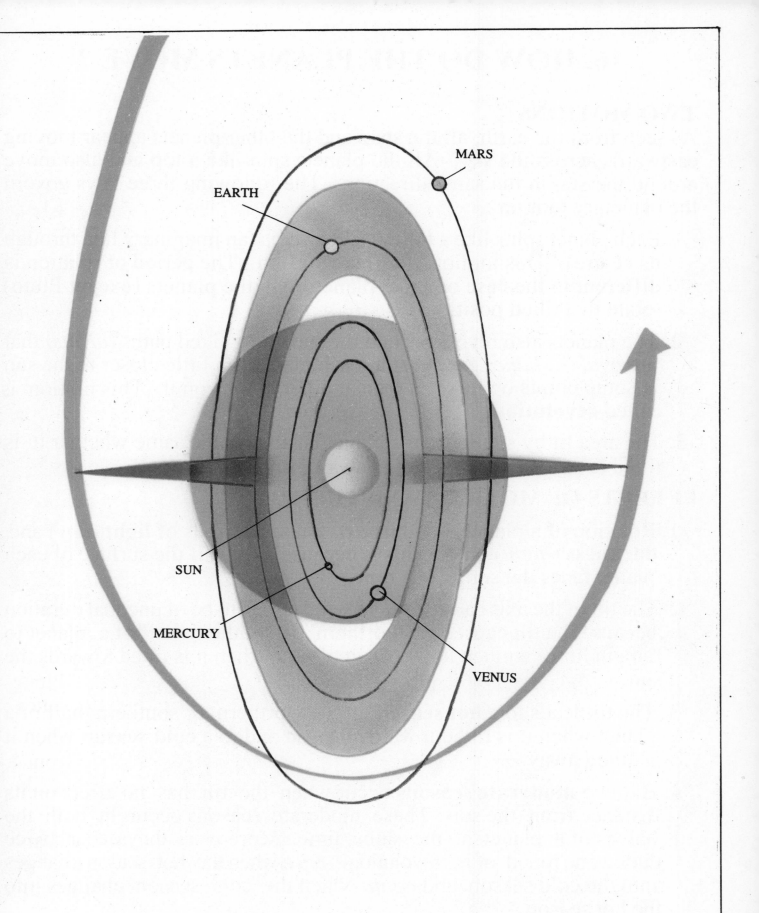

16. HOW DO THE PLANETS MOVE ?

TWO MOTIONS

As seen from the earth, all the stars and the other planets appear moving eastwards across the sky. All the planets spin like a top and also move around the sun in the same direction. The following three laws govern the planetary motion :

1. Each planet spins like a top around its axis (an imaginary line through its centre). This motion is called **rotation**. The period of rotation is different in the case of each planet. All the planets (except Pluto) rotate in a tilted position.

2. The planets also revolve round the sun along fixed paths (*orbits*) that are *oval in shape*. As a result, each planet is a little closer to the sun at some points on its orbit than at other points on it. This motion is called **revolution**.

3. The area lit by sunlight on a planet is always the same whether it is tilted towards the sun or tilted away from it.

EFFECTS OF MOTIONS AND THE TILT

1. Rotation of a planet round its *axis* causes periods of **light** (*day*) and **darkness** (*night*) on it. This is because only half the surface of each planet faces the sun at one time.

2. The tilt of the axis causes the days and nights to be of unequal duration because the tilt causes the northern or southern half of a planet to remain lit for a much longer span of time when it is tilted towards the sun.

3. The tilt leads to a **hot season** in the northern or southern half of a planet when it is tilted towards the sun and to a **cold season** when it is tilted away.

4. But two **moderate seasons** occur when the tilt has no effect on its distance from the sun. These moderate seasons occur in both the halves of a planet at the same time. Moreover, they occur twice during one round of its revolution—*once* when the hot season changes into the cold season and *again* when the cold season changes into the hot season.

HOW THE PLANETS MOVE

TOP

THE SPINNING
EARTH

FORMATION OF DAY AND NIGHT

NIGHT

DAY

DAY

NIGHT

SUN

SEASONS ON THE EARTH

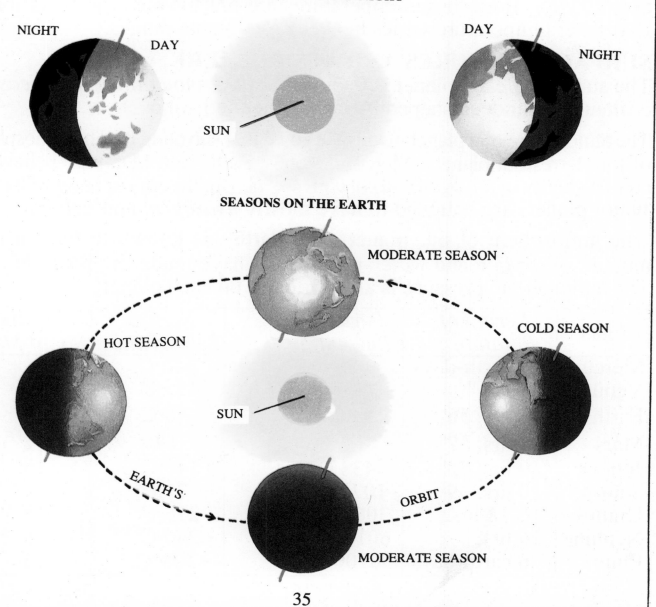

MODERATE SEASON

COLD SEASON

HOT SEASON

SUN

EARTH'S

ORBIT

MODERATE SEASON

17. MORE ABOUT PLANETS

DURATION OF ROTATION AND OF REVOLUTION

We know that planets differ in size. So, their periods of rotation are bound to be different. As a result, the length of days/nights cannot but differ too. Besides, each planet is at a different distance from the sun. So, it has a different period of its revolution round the sun. (See the table below).

TEMPERATURE

As the planets vary in terms of distance from the sun, they are bound to have different temperatures on them too. The planets nearer the sun are certainly hotter than those farther away from it. For example, the temperature on Mercury rises to about 342°C whereas that on Pluto falls to 223°C. Both these temperatures are not livable at all. As for the Earth, her temperature varies between the livable ranges.

SURFACE FEATURES AND ATMOSPHERE

The surface of each planet is believed to have *mountains, flat areas* and *craters*. It is indeed shaped by its weather and atmosphere.

The atmosphere of a planet means the gases that surround it. The atmospheres of four terrestrial planets (Mercury, Venus, Earth, and Mars) are believed to consist chiefly of *nitrogen* and *carbon dioxide*. But the atmospheres of the four major planets are believed to have mostly *hydrogen* and *helium*.

The atmosphere of our planet—the Earth—is known to have a large amount of *oxygen* and *water-vapour* that have made life possible on it. The atmospheric pressure is also different on each planet.

Planet	Period of Rotation	Period of Revolution	Surface Temperature	Maximum No. of Moons
Mercury	59 earth-days	88 earth-days	342°C	—
Venus	243 "	225 "	455°C	—
Earth	23 hrs. 56'	365 "	58°C	1
Mars	24 hrs. 37'	687 "	−31°C	2
Jupiter	9 hrs. 55'	4333 "	−149°C	16
Saturn	10 hrs. 39'	10759 "	−176°C	24
Uranus	16-18 hrs.	30685 "	−216°C	15
Neptune	16 hrs.	60188 "	−240°C	8
Pluto	6 earth-days	90700 "	−208°C	1

JUPITER

EARTH

VENUS

18. MERCURY—THE HOTTEST PLANET

BASIC FACTS

Mercury is the planet nearest the sun. It is quite smaller than the earth. Because of its nearness to the sun, it is hard to see it in bright sunlight without a telescope. But sometimes it can be seen in the western sky at sunset. That is why it is called the **Evening Star** also.

Mercury completes one rotation around its axis in about 59 earth-days. Till 1965, astronomers believed that this planet completed its revolution in 88 days—the period in which it completes one revolution round the sun. Because of its slow rotation and very fast revolution, its solar day lasts 176 earth-days.

SPECIAL FEATURES

Photographs of Mercury show that it has a rocky surface just like the moon's. Again, it reflects 6% of the sunlight it receives just as the moon does. It has broad flat plains, steep cliffs and deep craters on its surface. As for the interior of Mercury, it is like that of the earth. It consists of iron and some other heavy elements. Also, it has a magnetic field around it. Mercury is a dry and almost airless planet. On it the sun appears about 2·5 times as big as it appears on the earth and the temperature may reach 342°C during the day. At night, it may drop to about — 193°C. It all happens because of a weak atmosphere.

On this planet, the sky looks black and the stars can be seen by day too. The atmosphere around Mercury consists of a small amount of *helium, hydrogen* and *oxygen*. Still it is very thin and weak. Life is not possible on Mercury because of its very high temperature and insufficient oxygen.

IN MYTHOLOGY

In Roman mythology, Mercury was the messenger of gods. He was the god of *roads, travel, commerce, property* and *wealth*. The words—**merchant, commerce** and **merchandise** are related to it. Its ancient symbol is ☿

Children ! you must have read the story—*The Honest Woodcutter*. The angel (god) that appeared before the woodcutter when his axe had fallen into the river was none else but Mercury.

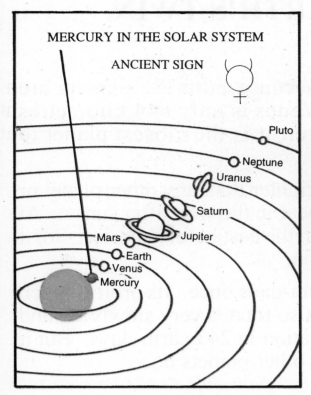

MERCURY IN THE SOLAR SYSTEM

ANCIENT SIGN

Pluto
Neptune
Uranus
Saturn
Jupiter
Mars
Earth
Venus
Mercury

MERCURY—GOD OF WEALTH

MERCURY—THE PLANET

19. VENUS—THE EARTH'S TWIN

BASIC FACTS

Venus is known as the Earth's twin because both the planets are very similar in size. The diameter of Venus is only 644 kilometres smaller than that of the earth. Moreover, it is the closest planet to the earth.

When seen from the earth, Venus looks brighter than any other planet or star. Sometimes it is the first planet to appear in the west after sunset. At other times, it is the last planet to be seen in the east before sunrise. So, it is called the *Evening Star/Morning Star* too.

Venus goes round the sun in about 225 earth-days once. Its orbit is much less oval than that of any other planet. It also rotates very slowly around its axis and completes its one round of rotation in 243 earth-days. But it rotates in the direction opposite to that all other planets do.

SPECIAL FEATURES

The surface of Venus is also very hot and dry. It has varying surface-features—*mountains, flat plains, canyons* and *valleys.* It has two huge mountainous regions on it. The surface of this planet is either dusty or covered with sharp-edged rocks.

Venus has no water on its surface which is very hot and dry. It is covered with thick clouds made up of mainly carbon dioxide. Besides, it has small amounts of nitrogen, water-vapour and some other gases like sulphur dioxide. The air-pressure is much heavier on Venus than on the Earth. Beneath the thick clouds, the sky looks orange-coloured. Flashes of lightning also occur. In the sky of this planet the clouds have sulphuric acid in them showing that there are active volcanoes on this planet. It has the largest volcano in the entire Solar System. It rises 25 kilometres high and is named **Olympus Mons.**

Venus has a maximum surface temperature of about 455°C—hotter than most ovens even. Life is not possible on it because of its high temperature and lack of oxygen in its air-coat.

IN MYTHOLOGY

In Roman mythology, Venus is the goddess of *love, beauty* and *creative force.* Her son—*Cupid*—is the god of love. Its ancient sign is ♀

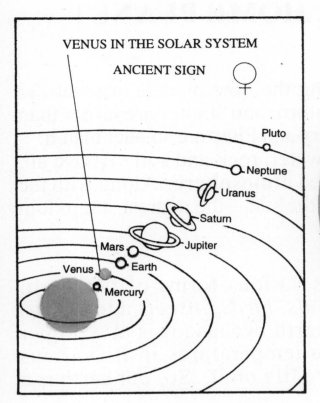

VENUS IN THE SOLAR SYSTEM

ANCIENT SIGN

Pluto

Neptune

Uranus

Saturn

Jupiter

Mars

Venus

Earth

Mercury

VENUS—GODDESS OF LOVE

VENUS—THE PLANET

UNLIKE OTHER PLANETS, VENUS ROTATES IN THE OPPOSITE DIRECTION—EAST TO WEST

20. THE EARTH---OUR HOME PLANET

BASIC FACTS
The earth stands just in the middle among the nine planets in regard to size. Four planets—Uranus, Neptune, Saturn, and Jupiter are larger than it while four of them—Mars, Venus, Mercury and Pluto are smaller than it. The earth is a huge sphere covered with water, rock and soil. Above all, it is surrounded by a coat of air that is called **atmosphere**. Along with the other eight planets, it also revolves round the sun—the nearest star to it in the galaxy called the Milky Way.

A UNIQUE PLANET
The earth is our home-planet and has various forms of life on it. This life includes *human-beings, animals, birds, insects* and *plants*. These forms of life are found on the earth because it is at a proper distance from the sun and has livable temperatures in its various parts. No other planet is known to have life on it. So, our earth is a unique planet in this respect.

SPECIAL FEATURES
The earth's crust is made of rock. It is under water or soil. Beneath the crust, the earth is very hot. The earth is constantly spinning like a top from west to east. At the same time, it is revolving around the sun. The two motions are called **rotation** and **revolution** respectively.

Rotation of the earth causes days and nights on it while its revolution, coupled with the tilt in its axis, leads to changes in season and difference in the lengths of the *day* and the *night.*

Study of the earth is called **geology**. The atmosphere of the earth contains enough oxygen to support animal life. This gas is highly active and forms about 21% of the atmosphere. About 78% of it is nitrogen. The remaining 1% of it has dust, water-vapour and other gases—carbon dioxide, argon etc.

There are three layers of the earth below its crust—*mantle, outer core* and *inner core.* The molten metal forms its inner core. It keeps moving and producing electricity inside the earth. This electricity has made the earth a big magnet with a strong force of gravity. The earth is believed to be 4500 million years old. It has only one moon. Its ancient sign is ⊕

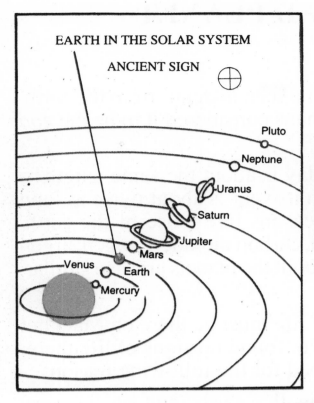

EARTH IN THE SOLAR SYSTEM

ANCIENT SIGN ⊕

Pluto
Neptune
Uranus
Saturn
Jupiter
Mars
Venus
Earth
Mercury

THE EARTH—OUR HOME PLANET

THE EARTH'S FACE

43

21. MARS—THE RED PLANET

BASIC FACTS

Mars is the only planet whose surface can be seen in detail from the earth. It is reddish in colour and the ancient Romans considered it to be the *god of war*.

Mars is like the earth in some ways. Its day is about the same length as the earth's *(24 hours 37·5 minutes)* though its year is about twice as long *(687 days)*. It has summer and winter seasons like those of the earth. Moreover, its atmosphere contains nitrogen, carbon dioxide, oxygen, argon and water-vapour. The surface features of both the planets are also similar.

SPECIAL FEATURES

People in the past believed that intelligent life must be there on Mars but the space-craft, that landed on Mars in 1976, found no signs of life there. Life would not be easy on this planet indeed for the following reasons :

1. Mars is much farther from the sun than the earth and so has very low temperatures (—124°C to —24°C).

2. The atmosphere of Mars is too thin to block the sun's harmful radiation.

3. Its atmosphere contains a high percentage of carbon dioxide and it is not possible to breathe in it.

It is believed that Mars had large amounts of surface water millions of years ago ; but almost none exists at present. It may be there in frozen state in its polar areas or beneath the crust of this planet.

The surface of Mars has bright areas, dark areas and polar areas but no oceans. Craters, deep gorges and river-beds are also visible on Mars through a telescope.

Mars has two moons whereas our earth has only one. They appear as dots to its *left* and *right* respectively.

Between Mars and Jupiter there are thousands of mini-planets that are called **asteroids**.

IN MYTHOLOGY

In mythology, Mars was believed to be the **god of conflict/war.** Its ancient sign is ♂

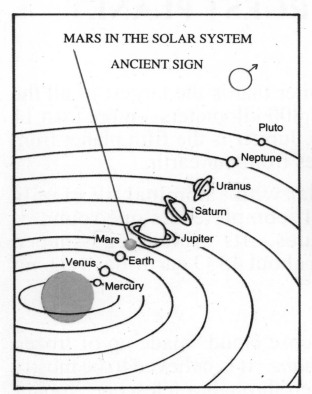

MARS IN THE SOLAR SYSTEM

ANCIENT SIGN

Pluto
Neptune
Uranus
Saturn
Jupiter
Mars
Earth
Venus
Mercury

MARS—GOD OF WAR

MARS—THE PLANET

TWO MOONS OF MARS

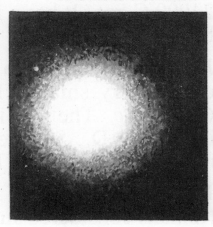

45

22. JUPITER—THE LARGEST PLANET

BASIC FACTS

Across the asteroid belt is the planet Jupiter that is the largest of all the planets. It has a diameter measuring 142,800 kilometers—more than 11 times that of the earth. In terms of order, Jupiter is the fifth planet from the sun. It is about 629 million kilometres from our earth.

Jupiter has its axis almost perpendicular with a nominal tilt of only 3°. It is a very fast spinning planet. It completes its one round of rotation in only 9 hours and 55 minutes. Its orbit is egg-shaped (oval) and it goes once round the sun in about 4333 earth-days (about 12 earth-years).

SPECIAL FEATURES

The Jupiter is surrounded by layers of dense clouds made up of frozen crystals of two gases—*ammonia* and *methane*. It is believed to be mostly gaseous and nominally liquid. When seen through a telescope, Jupiter appears with a series of belts of dark lines across its surface parallel to its equator. These belts keep changing their positions and the zones between them are light coloured. A large oval mark—*Great Red Spot*—can also be seen on its surface.

Jupiter's atmosphere consists of 84% hydrogen, 15% helium and 1% other gases. Its core is believed to have an iron-bearing solid rock about the size of our earth.

The top of Jupiter's clouds has an average temperature of 149°C. Beneath them, it rises higher and higher to reach about 2900°C. But the surface temperature has not been determined so far. Its central core may be about 24000°C hot. It has a faint ring around it which was discovered in 1979 by Voyager I.

Jupiter has 16 known moons, four of them being very large while the others very small. These four moons are *Europa, Io, Callisto* and *Ganymede*. The four large moons of Jupiter were discovered by Galileo in 1610 A.D. So, they are known as *Galilean Moons* too. Very fast rotation of this planet leads to very high winds on it.

IN MYTHOLOGY

Romans considered Jupiter to be the **king of gods**. Its ancient sign is ♃

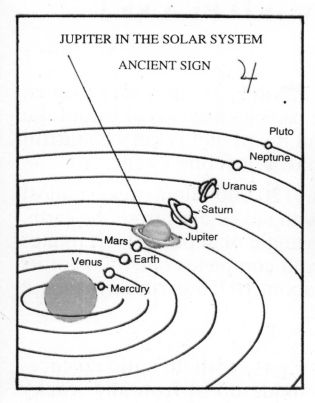

JUPITER IN THE SOLAR SYSTEM

ANCIENT SIGN

Pluto
Neptune
Uranus
Saturn
Jupiter
Mars
Earth
Venus
Mercury

JUPITER—KING OF GODS

JUPITER—THE PLANET

FOUR CHIEF MOONS OF JUPITER

23. SATURN—THE RINGED PLANET

BASIC FACTS

Saturn is the second largest planet after Jupiter. It has a set of seven thin rings around it. They are made up of ice-particles that travel round the planet. The rings emit a shine as well and the planet is very beautiful to look at. They can be seen with a small telescope even.

This planet has a diameter measuring about 120,000 kilometres—almost 10 times that of the earth. It can be seen with naked eyes from the earth. Saturn has an oval orbit. Its axis tilts at an angle of about 27°. It rotates faster than any other planet except Jupiter. It completes one round of its rotation in 10 hours 39 minutes. It takes about 10759 earth-days (about 29.5 earth-years) to go round the sun once.

SPECIAL FEATURES

It is believed that Saturn is a giant ball of gas, with no solid surface. But it may have a hot solid inner core made up of iron and rocky material. The outer core around this inner core consists of ammonia, methane and water. About this outer core is a mantle of compressed liquid hydrogen. And around this layer is a coat composed of hydrogen and helium.

The upper layers of this hydrogen and helium become gaseous and merge with the atmosphere of the planet as it too consists of these very two gases. Over all, Saturn is covered by a layer of thick clouds.

Scientists are not sure about any life on this planet. It has changing seasons each of which lasts about 7.5 earth-years. The temperature above the clouds is averagely −176° C. It goes on increasing below the clouds.

Saturn has 23 moons the largest of which is *Titan*. It was discovered in 1655 A.D. It is the only moon known to have an atmosphere in the entire solar system.

IN MYTHOLOGY

In Roman mythology, Saturn was considered as the god of fertility and agriculture. At first this god had its separate identity. But later on, it came to be identified with Greek god named Cronus. Saturn's wife Ops was also the goddess of harvest. Saturn's ancient symbol is ♄

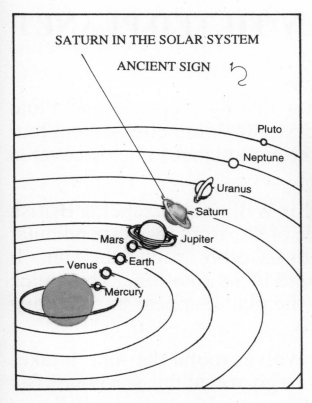

SATURN IN THE SOLAR SYSTEM

ANCIENT SIGN ♄

Pluto
Neptune
Uranus
Saturn
Mars
Jupiter
Venus
Earth
Mercury

SATURN—GOD OF FERTILITY

SATURN—THE PLANET

TITAN

ICE-PARTICLES IN RINGS OF THE SATURN

49

24. URANUS—THE HIGHLY TILTED PLANET

BASIC FACTS

Uranus is the seventh planet from the sun with only Neptune and Pluto further away. It has a diameter measuring 51, 800 kilometres—about four times the diameter of the earth. It was the first planet to be discovered with a telescope.

Uranus was discovered in 1781 A.D. by Sir William Herschel, a British astronomer. It has its axis tilted at an angle of 98° from the perpendicular position so that it is almost in level with its orbit around the sun. It takes only 17 hours to complete one round of its rotation. This quick rotation and the large angle of tilt make the planet appear to roll along in its orbit.

Uranus has an oval orbit along which it revolves round the sun. It takes about 30,685 earth-days (84 earth-years) to go round the sun once. But little is known so far about the surface of Uranus. However, it is believed that Uranus is surrounded by clouds. Its average temperature is −216° C.

SPECIAL FEATURES

When viewed through the best telescope, Uranus appears as a ball of gas, bluish in colour. This colour is because of the methane gas that is there along with hydrogen and helium in its atmosphere.

Uranus has at least 13 very faint rings around it. They consist of countless chunks of a black material which is not known till now. Uranus has 15 known moons. Till 1986, only five of its moons were known. But the U.S. spacecraft Voyager II discovered 10 other moons in that year.

IN MYTHOLOGY

In Roman mythology, Uranus was the earliest god. He was known to be the husband of goddess *Gea*—the earth. The couple begot children that were known as *Titans* in mythology. There was a serious quarrel between the couple over their children and Gea (Earth) became separate from Uranus. After this separation Uranus lost its importance in mythology and his functions were taken over by his grandosn *Zeus*. The ancient symbol of Uranus is

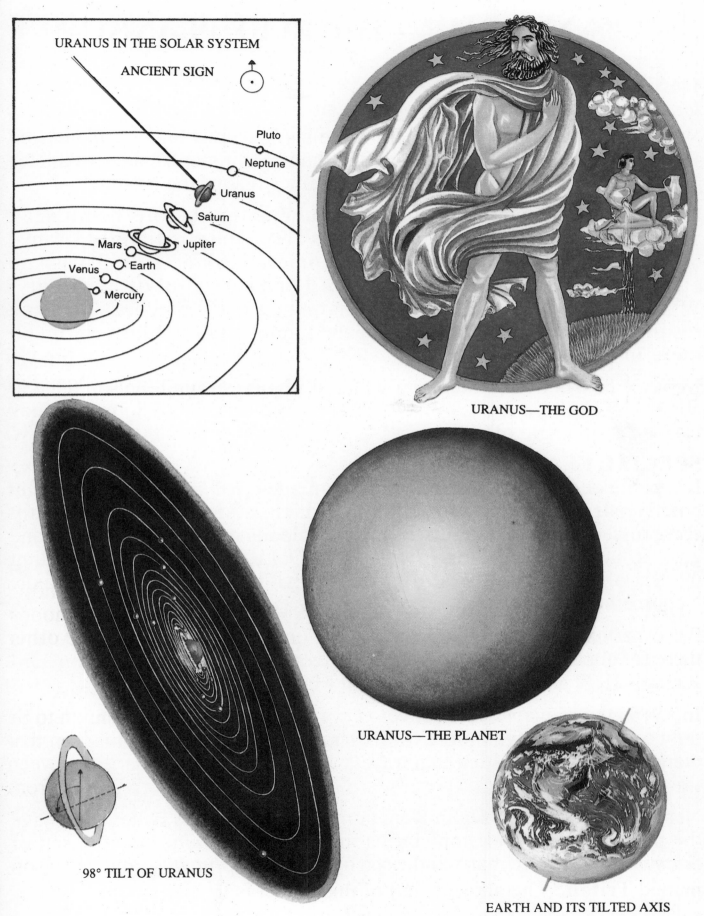

URANUS IN THE SOLAR SYSTEM

ANCIENT SIGN

Pluto

Neptune

Uranus

Saturn

Mars

Jupiter

Venus

Earth

Mercury

URANUS—THE GOD

URANUS—THE PLANET

98° TILT OF URANUS

EARTH AND ITS TILTED AXIS

51

25. NEPTUNE—THE BLUE PLANET

BASIC FACTS

Neptune is the farthest planet from the sun except Pluto. It cannot be seen without a telescope. It is smaller than Uranus and has a diameter measuring 49,500 kilometres—about 4 times that of the earth.

Neptune was discovered through mathematics before being seen through a telescope. When predictions about the positions of Uranus on certain times went wrong, astronomers became sure that some other planet disturbs the positions of Uranus by dint of its gravity. When John C. Adams, a British mathematician, reached the same result, the astronomers looked for the planet and found it very much there in 1846 A.D.

Neptune has an oval orbit along which it revolves round the sun once in about 165 earth-years. It rotates round its axis once in 16 hours. Its axis is tilted at an angle of 30°.

SPECIAL FEATURES

It is believed that Neptune is a gas-giant made up of *hydrogen* and *helium* chiefly. It has a central rocky core which is surrounded by heavily compressed gases in the form of moving clouds made of frozen methane gas. It has a big dark area. This *Great Dark Spot* consists of swirling masses of gas and is the size of our earth. Due to the tilt of its axis, Neptune has seasons on it.

Pluto moves inside the Neptune's orbit once in 248 years. It remains there for about 20 years. This time Pluto entered Neptune's orbit on 23rd January 1979 and will remain in it till March 15, 1999 A.D.

In 1989, the Voyager II discovered six new moons of Neptune though only two were known before it. Its largest moon is *Triton*. It is the only planet in our solar system that travels **east to west**.

IN MYTHOLOGY

Neptune is the god of sea in Roman mythology. It was believed to have the power to start and stop storms in oceans. Neptune was the son of *Saturn* and *Ops*. He married the sea nymph—*Amphitrite*—and had a son named **Triton**. The ancient sign of this planet is ♆

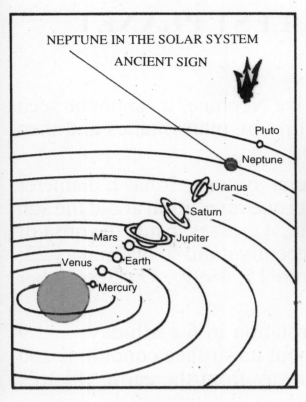

NEPTUNE IN THE SOLAR SYSTEM
ANCIENT SIGN

Pluto
Neptune
Uranus
Saturn
Mars
Jupiter
Venus
Earth
Mercury

NEPTUNE—GOD OF STORMS

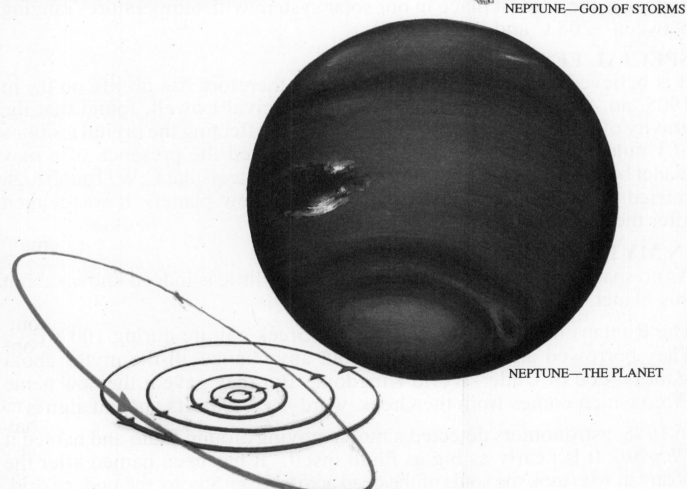

NEPTUNE—THE PLANET

PLUTO INSIDE THE ORBIT OF NEPTUNE

26. PLUTO—THE SMALLEST PLANET

BASIC FACTS

Pluto is the farthest planet from the sun. Like Neptune, it cannot be seen with naked eyes. It was also discovered first by mathematics and then located through the telescope in 1930 A.D.

Pluto has an ovalmost orbit in the entire solar system. It has a diameter measuring 2285 kilometres. It completes its one revolution about the sun in 248 years. When it comes nearest the sun, it crosses inside the orbit of Neptune and remains there for 20 years. Recently it did so on January 23, 1979 A.D. and will remain there till March 15, 1999. On September 12,1979, it was nearest the sun.

As for rotation, Pluto completes its one rotation in 6 earth-days and 9 hours. Astronomers do not know much about its surface conditions and its exact size because it is very, very far away from the earth. Pluto's surface is the coldest place in our solar system with temperatures ranging between −208°C and −323°C.

SPECIAL FEATURES

It is believed that Pluto is mainly icy and therefore has no life on it. In 1905, an Amercian astronomer, named Percival Lowell, found that the gravity of some unknown heavenly body was affecting the orbital motions of Uranus and Neptune. In 1915, he predicted the presence of a new planet beyond Neptune. He died in 1916 but his assistant C.W. Taunbaugh carried on the search and in 1930 located a new planet. It was named after the Roman god of the Dead—*Pluto*.

IN MYTHOLOGY

As no spacecraft has visited Pluto so far, very little is indeed known about this planet.

The Romans had come in contact with Greek culture during 100's B.C. They borrowed and preserved without any change all the myths about *Hades*—god of Under-World Kingdom. But they gave it the new name *Pluto* which comes from the Greek word—*Plouton.* Its ancient sign is ♏

In 1978, astronomers detected a moon moving around Pluto and named it *Charon*. It is nearly as big as Pluto inself. It has been named after the boatman who took the souls of the dead across *River Styx* to the underworld.

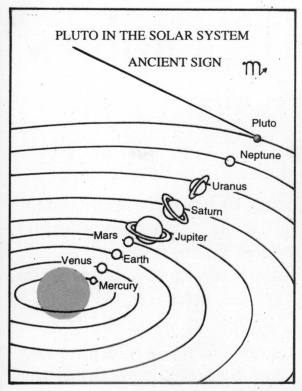

PLUTO IN THE SOLAR SYSTEM

ANCIENT SIGN ♏

Pluto

Neptune

Uranus

Saturn

Mars

Jupiter

Venus

Earth

Mercury

PLUTO—GOD OF THE UNDER-WORLD

PLUTO—THE PLANET

CHARON—PLUTO'S MOON

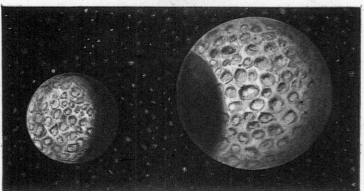

UNIT V
SATELLITES AND OTHER BODIES

27. NATURAL SATELLITES (MOONS)

The word **satellite** has come down from the Latin word *satellitis* which means *attendant* or *secondary*. So, we can define a satellite as under :

A satellite is a body that revolves round another (bigger) body in space. Our moon is the satellite of our earth. Similarly, six other planets in the solar system have their moons. Only Mercury and Venus have none. The Earth and Pluto have just one moon each while Mars has two. Neptune has 8 moons whereas Jupiter, Saturn and Uranus have 16, 23 and 15 respectively.

It must also be remembered that there is every chance of more undiscovered satellites (moons) to be located around the outer planets. Besides, the smallest moon is that of Mars *(Deimos)* which is only 12 kilometres across. As for the largest moon, it is that of Jupiter *(Ganymede)* with a diameter measuring 5262 kilometres.

Apart from the satellites circling the planets, there are dark bodies that revolve around certain stars and either dim or brighten their lights. These bodies are also called satellites. The table given below shows the number of satellites that circle seven of the nine planets in our solar system.

Planets	No. of Moons	Planets	No. of Moons
Mercury	-	Saturn	23
Venus	-	Uranus	15
Earth	1	Neptune	8
Mars	2	Pluto	1
Jupiter	16	—	—

How was the moon (Earth's satellite) formed ? One theory explains that the earth collided with some other body and as a result, some *debris* was scattered into space. Due to the earth's gravity, the debris began to revolve round the earth. Slowly it began to collect together and the result was **our moon**. May be, most of the moons have been formed in a similar way.

FORMATION OF THE EARTH'S MOON

28. ASTEROIDS

An **asteroid** *is a very small heavenly body that revolves round the sun.* It is also called a **planetoid** *(minor planet).*

Most of the asteroids are found in the wide gap between the orbits of Mars and Jupiter. These asteroids occur as a belt shown in the picture below. The largest asteroid is **Ceres** which is about 1000 kilometres across. It was discovered on January 1, 1801 A.D. It must be remembered that asteroids have very irregular surfaces and shapes. Also, they have unusual orbits to circle round the sun.

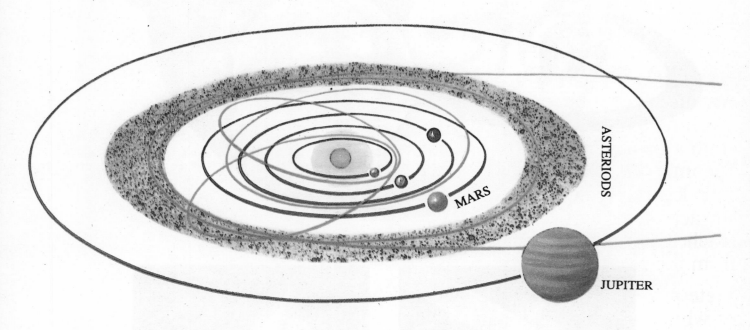

There are thousands of known asteroids. About 30,000 of them shine brightly at times to be photographed. Astronomers know about the orbits of about 4000 of them.

Gravity of Jupiter keeps constantly affecting the orbits of asteroids. It may lead to collisions and chain-collisions. As a result, still smaller asteroids may be formed. The closest recorded collision took place on March 22, 1989 A.D. Most of the asteroids are believed to have been formed when dust-specks circling the sun took the shape of small clumps. These clumps, then, collected together and grew in size.

29. METEORS

A **meteor** is a bright streak of light seen in the sky for a very short time. So, it is also called a *shooting star* or *falling star* because it looks like a star falling from the sky.

A meteor is indeed a chunk of metallic or rocky matter that enters the earth's atmosphere from space. This matter is called a **meteoroid.** Friction of the air makes it so hot that it glows and leaves a trail of hot glowing gases behind it.

Astronomers believe that about 200 million visible meteors enter the earth's air-coat every day. A meteor becomes visible when it is about 105 kilometres away from the surface of the earth. By the time it reaches between 50 to 80 kilometres from the earth, it has caught fire.

Meteors belong to the solar system of which our earth is a part. They move faster than the earth does. When they have entered the earth's atmosphere, their speed increases considerably.

Most of the meteors are the size of a sand-grain and burn for a few seconds only. But the trail of a meteor lasts a good few minutes.

The picture given in front shows a meteor approaching the surface of the earth.

An invisible meteoroid travels through outer space, which has no atmosphere.

The thin air of the upper atmosphere begins to heat the object, causing it to glow and create a trail of hot gases.

Friction of denser atmosphere makes the object burn at white heat and become visible as a meteor.

The object usually breaks, and burns up completely before reaching the ground.

A meteor appears in the sky whenever an object called a meteoroid hurtles into the earth's atmosphere from space.

30. METEORITES

A. **meteorite** is a meteor-like body in space. It is large enough to reach the earth's surface without burning up in the atmosphere (unlike a meteor).

While falling, a meteorite leaves a bright trail in the sky. This trail is known as a **fire-ball**. It is hard to locate a meteorite even if the trail is followed because it looks just like an ordinary stone. So, it cannot be easily distinguished.

A meteorite may be made of *metal* (iron and nickel) or *stone*. It may be a fragment from colliding asteroids. In 1908, a meteorite—*Tunguska*—crashed on the ground in Siberia. Its blast was felt by people up to a distance of 80 kilometres.

Scientists collect meteorites to study their material in order to know more and more about the material of which planets are made.

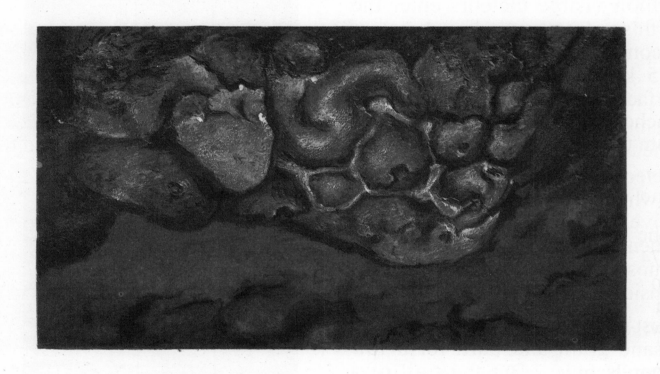

When a meteorite crashes on the earth, it causes a crater—deep pit—that may be several kilometres across. The meteor-crater caused by the smashing of the meteorite *Barringer* is 1265 metres across and 174 metres deep. It can be seen in the Arizona Desert in USA.

31. COMETS

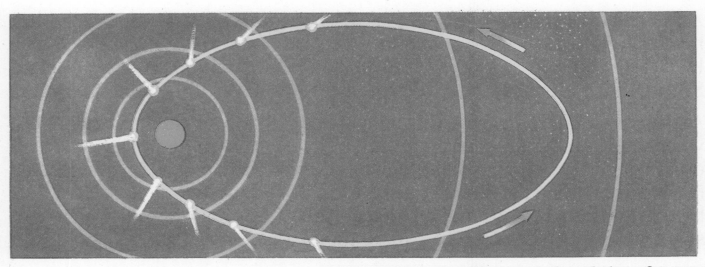

Comets are believed to be left-over particles of the gas cloud that formed the solar system. This left-over gas cloud contains billions of icy lumps. Each lump is a comet with a nucleus made up of crumbly rock-particles trapped inside a frozen liquid.

Any time a comet may be knocked off its normal course and move towards the sun. Getting near it, its outer icy part melts and boils away into vapour. As for the solid inner part, it is released of the icy trap as dust. Thus the comet forms an enormous head with a long tail. As it travels in space, it sheds bits of itself. The picture given above clearly shows a travelling comet. When the comet travels away from the sun, its tail gets shorter and it again becomes a snowball. Moreover, it always travels tail first.

The English scientist Edmund Halley (1656-1742) A.D. became famous for his research on comets. He proved that the comets seen in 1531 A.D., 1607 A.D. and in 1628 A.D. (which he himself saw) were the same one comet. He predicted that it will be seen in 1759 A.D. again and it happened so. So, it was named **Comet Halley**. Remember that this comet has been seen in 1835 A.D., 1910 A.D. and 1986 A.D. again and again. According to Halley, it will be seen 2300 times more and then decay.

HALLEY'S COMET

EDMUND HALLEY

32. ARTIFICIAL SATELLITES

An **artificial satellite** is a space-craft shot into space to make it orbit a heavenly body—*planet* or *moon* etc. The first artificial satellite was launched from the earth by USSR on October 4, 1957 A.D. It was named **Sputnik I**. Since then hundreds of satellites have been sent into space.

Artificial satellities are of different types. Some of them tell us about weather while others point out the area with mineral deposits etc. Still others provide us with instant telephone calls or help us watch the events happening around the world (live) on our TV-sets. Not only this, satellites help astronomers with much needed space-information. They also help ships and aeroplanes to know about their exact positions.

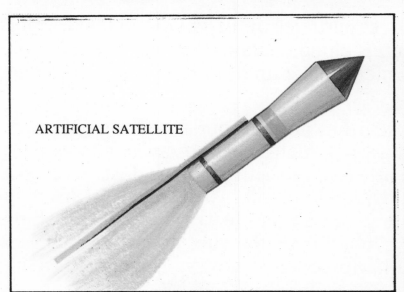

ARTIFICIAL SATELLITE

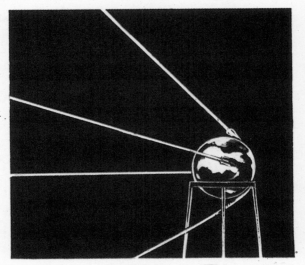

SPACE INFORMATION COMING TO THE EARTH

Each satellite comes to occupy a special orbit around the earth. It is called a **geo-stationary orbit**. If a satellite is there about 3600 kilometres away from the earth, it orbits the earth in about 24 hours—period for the earth's own one rotation-round. So, it appears *stationary* in the sky. The electric power needed for the satellite to work comes from **solar cells** that convert sunlight into electricity. Rocket motors called **trusters** keep the satellite in the correct position so that its dish-aerials point to the earth.

The earth's gravity makes a satellite stay in its orbit. Without it, it is sure to drift into space in a straight line.

While launching a satellite, its rockets must be controlled carefully to give it the required speed to go up—about 11,100 kilometres an hour.

SATELLITE ORBITING THE EARTH

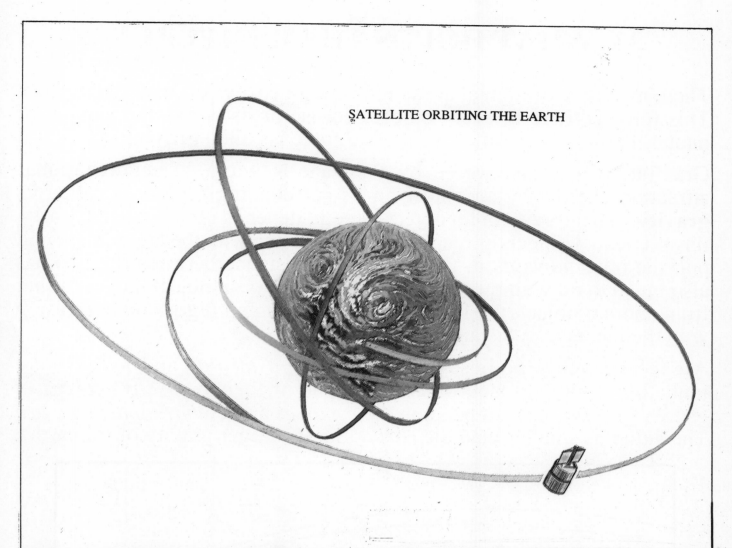

SATELLITE SHOOTING OFF THE EARTH

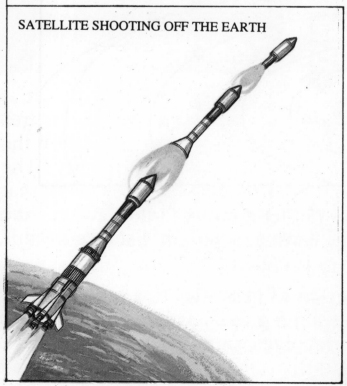

SATELLITE SENDING INFORMATION TO THE EARTH

33. WHAT HOLDS THEM IN PLACE ?

There is a force of mutual attraction acting between all material objects. This force is there in every object because of its *mass*—the amount of matter that it is made of. This mutual force is called **gravitation**.

Gravitation was discovered by Sir Isaac Newton. The gravitational attraction exerted by an object on its surrounding objects is called its **gravity**. The gravity of an object directly depends on its *mass*. Clearly, if two unequal objects attract each other, the one with the larger mass will pull the other towards it. Moreover, the distance between the two has also much to do with this force of attraction. As an object moves farther from another object, the force of gravity acting on it goes on decreasing with the increase in distance.

All the heavenly bodies—*stars, planets, asteroids* and *moons*—are mutually attracting each other by means of their *respective forces of gravity*. These forces depend on their *masses* and on *how apart they are*. The *moon* is smaller than the *earth*. So, the larger gravity of the earth

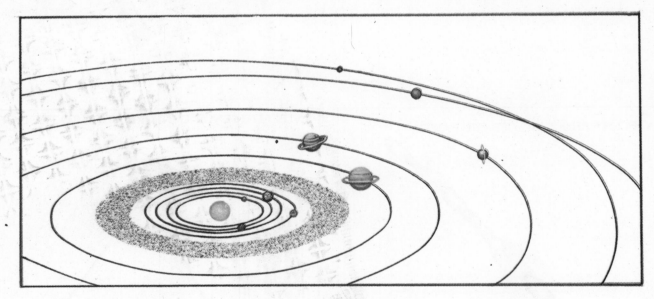

overcomes its lesser gravity and does not let it move farther away. As a result, it is forced to revolve round the earth at a certain distance from it. The path along which the moon moves is called its *orbit*.

It is this principle of **mutual interaction of gravities** that holds various heavenly bodies in their places. The sun's gravity is larger than that of any of the planets. So, each of them revolves round it.